MONKEYS

BY HERBERT S. ZIM

ILLUSTRATED BY GARDELL D. CHRISTENSEN

WILLIAM MORROW AND COMPANY, NEW YORK, 1955

The author is grateful for aid received from those with expert competence, especially from the National Zoological Park, Washington, D. C. His special thanks also go to Dr. Donald Hoffmeister, University of Illinois, Urbana, Illinois; and Mr. Ernest Ediger, formerly of The Monkey Jungle, Miami, Florida.

· · · · · · · ·

Of all the thousands of kinds of animals, monkeys are the most fun. Next time you go to the zoo take your eyes off the monkeys for a minute and watch the people who are watching the monkeys. See how they hold their breath when a monkey makes a daring leap. Listen to them laugh when the monkeys play tricks on each other. It is easy to see why people like monkeys. In many ways they look and act like small, wild living cartoons of human beings.

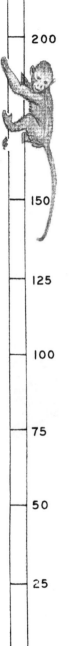

225 MONKEYS

200

150

125

100

75

50

25

There are good reasons why monkeys remind us of ourselves. They belong to a large group, or order, of mammals—the primates—and so do we. Apes and lemurs also are primates, but there are more kinds of monkeys in the primate group than all the other primates put together. There are about 225 different species, or kinds, of monkeys; about 75 kinds of lemurs; about 14 kinds of great apes; and only one species of man.

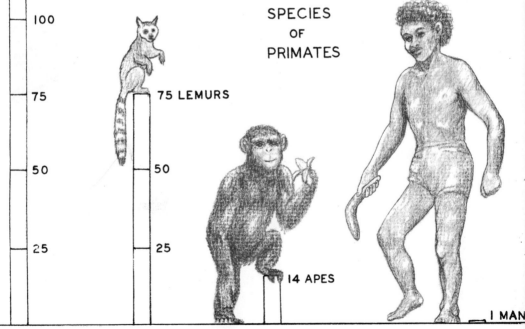

SPECIES
OF
PRIMATES

75 LEMURS

50

25

14 APES

1 MAN

The primates differ greatly in size and appearance. Some live in trees, some on the ground. Most have tails; a few do not. One thing about all primates is their unusual hands or feet, which are different from those of all other animals. The big toe, or thumb, of some primates (including human beings, all apes, and some monkeys) sticks out at a wide angle.

MAN

CHIMPANZEE

COLOBUS MONKEY

CAPUCHIN MONKEY

MARMOSET

EASTERN GRAY SQUIRREL

MOUSE

BLACK BEAR

RACCOON

HANDS AND PAWS
1/5TH ACTUAL SIZE

TIGER

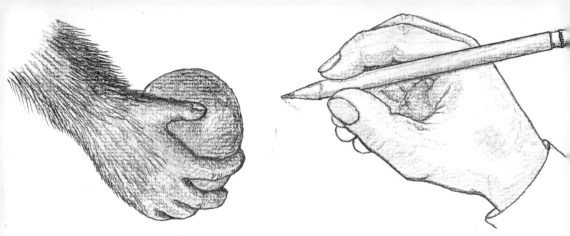

These primates can move the thumb so it can touch all the other toes or fingers of that hand or foot. Such a hand, with an opposable thumb, can be used for grasping. It can hold a branch, a piece of fruit, or even a tool. Some primates, including monkeys, can grasp equally well with hands or with feet.

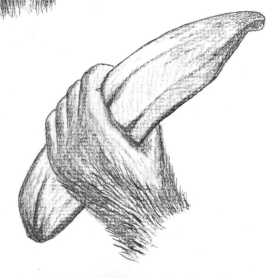

If you look closely at the fingers and toes of primates you will see that most of them have flattened nails instead of the claws that many other animals have.

Primates have teeth that permit them to eat both plant and animal food. They are active animals with good eyesight, a keen sense of smell, and well-developed brains. Most are found in warm lands, but a few live where winters are cold. Many prefer to live in trees. Primates nearly always stay in a family group. They are social animals and rarely live alone.

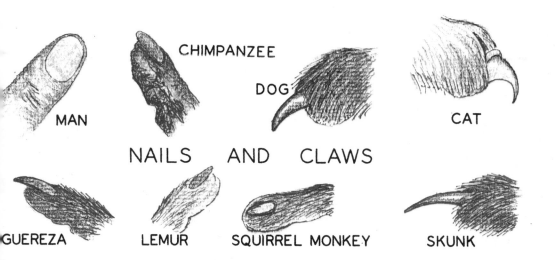

MAN   CHIMPANZEE   DOG   CAT

NAILS   AND   CLAWS

GUEREZA   LEMUR   SQUIRREL MONKEY   SKUNK

SOOTY MANGABYS

The great apes, sometimes called monkeys by mistake, make up one small but distinct group of primates. They are probably the most interesting animals in the world for, as a group, they are most like people. Apes are very intelligent and seem to learn faster than any other primates except man. They live both in trees and on the ground. As they walk, climb, and feed, the great apes make excellent use of their almost human hands.

The long-armed, loose-jointed gibbon belongs to the ape family. A tree dweller of India,
Malaya, and the East Indies, it swings from
branch to branch on long, thin, strong arms.
The orangutan of Borneo and Malaya grows to
the size of a man. It is a long-armed, heavier,
clumsier tree dweller than the gibbon.

ORANGUTANS

Chimpanzees and gorillas are best known of the great apes. Chimps are about the size of a twelve-year-old boy. They are so lively and intelligent that people who raise them often treat young chimps like children. Gorillas are the largest primates. A full-grown, six-foot male may have a nine-foot arm spread and weigh over 600 pounds. Young gorillas are as friendly as chimps, but as they grow older, larger, and stronger, they become difficult to handle.

The primate group that includes the great apes also includes an odd group of much smaller animals, most of which live only on the island of Madagascar. These are the lemurs, which do not look or act much like monkeys. At night their weird cries and large shining eyes once made people think of ghosts. The lemurs and their rare relatives, the tarsiers, are the simplest primates. They are somewhat like tree shrews, small, insect-eating animals that are supposed to be very much like the long-extinct ancestors of all the primates.

MOUSE LEMUR

TARSIER

MAN

APES

OLD WORLD MONKEYS

NEW WORLD MONKEYS

LANGURS

MACAQUES

GUENONS

PREHENSILE

GUEREZA

NON PREHENSILE

BABOONS

MARMOSETS

LEMURS

FAMILY TREE
OF PRIMATES

TARSIERS

Now come the monkeys, a large group that is placed by scientists in two superfamilies with three distinct branches: the Old World monkeys, the New World monkeys, and the marmosets. These three groups of primates are the only groups that can truly be called monkeys. The names *Old World monkeys* and *New World*

ASIA

AUSTRALIA

LEGEND

NEW WORLD MONKEYS

OLD WORLD MONKEYS

LEMURS

monkeys tell where the two largest groups live. But there are other differences. Old World monkeys are much more like the great apes than the New World monkeys are. For example, these apes (and man) have 32 teeth. So do the Old World monkeys. The New World monkeys have 36 teeth.

The Old World monkeys have a narrow space between their nostrils, which open downward, like the nostrils of apes and of man. Depending on the species, their tails may be long or short. But none have a grasping, or prehensile, tail like those of some of the New World monkeys. Because their feet are hand-like, Old World monkeys can grasp things easily with them. Many have cheek pouches

16

NOSE CARTILAGE

NEW WORLD MONKEY
(SMOOTH-HEADED CAPUCHIN)

OLD WORLD MONKEY
(ROLOWAY)

ANUBIS BABOONS

into which they stuff food, to be chewed at leisure or in some safer place.

Old World monkeys have seat cushions formed from pads of tough skin. These odd patches of brightly colored skin are sometimes enlarged and swollen. Perhaps they make the monkeys seem more attractive to each other.

MANDRILL   **DRILL**

MONA GUENON is an active, restless forest monkey from around Nigeria.

VERVET GUENON of south-east and central Africa is about 25 inches long.

DIANA MONKEY is a handsome guenon with a crescent of white hair.

GREEN GUENON, often seen at zoos, has fur of a yellow-green hue.

MONKEYS

CRAB-EATING MACAQUES, of India and Malaya, can dive and swim.

WHITE-TAILED COLOBUS, or Guereza, is a tree dweller of the African mountains.

JAVA LANGUR is one of many leaf-eating monkeys in southeast Asia.

GELADA BABOON, with an odd, upturned nose, lives in low trees and amid rocks.

The Old World monkey group includes almost 150 species. Of course, they were known long before their New World relatives. You will certainly recognize the names of some of the monkeys in this group: baboons, mandrills, macaques (pronounced ma-kahk′), and guenons (pronounced guh-nawn′).

Baboons and mandrills are a bit doglike, both in their looks and in the way they walk. Some baboons have a heavy ridge across their foreheads, just above the eyes. This gives them an

GUINEA BABOONS

CHACMA BABOONS

SACRED, OR ARABIAN,
BABOON

angry, ferocious look. The males of the Arabian baboons have a fine mane of hair and are excellent fighters. Baboons were sacred to the Egyptians and many statues of them have been found in ancient temples.

The macaques are a group of some forty species. The best known is the rhesus (ree′-sus) monkey, widely used in laboratories and hospitals. The young rhesus makes a fairly good pet, because it is hardier than other monkeys. In some parts of Malaya, the pig-tailed macaque is trained to climb coconut palms, select ripe nuts, break them off, and throw them down to its owner.

The Barbary ape (not a member of the great ape group) belongs with the macaques too. Living at Gibraltar, it is the only monkey native to Europe. Several times the colony there has shrunk to only a few monkeys. When this has happened, the British, who hold Gibraltar, have added new animals. They are glad to do this to support the old legend that the British cannot be forced off the great armed rock as long as the Barbary apes are there.

BARBARY APES

The New World monkeys, found from Mexico south through the tropics of Brazil and Paraguay, include about 60 different species. As you can see from the family tree, they are a different branch of the monkey "family." New World monkeys have 36 teeth instead of 32.

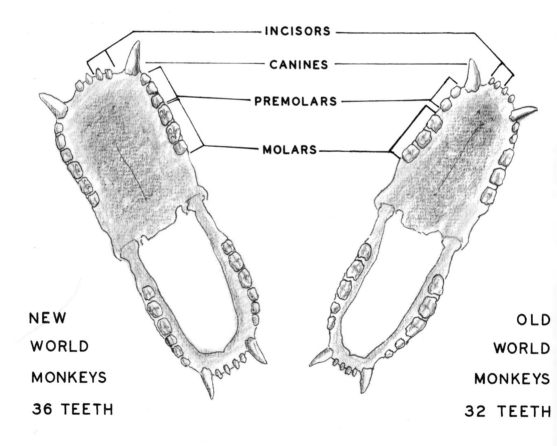

INCISORS

CANINES

PREMOLARS

MOLARS

NEW WORLD MONKEYS 36 TEETH

OLD WORLD MONKEYS 32 TEETH

VARIEGATED SPIDER MONKEYS

Their wide nostrils open to the front and sides, not downward. Their thumbs are not so useful in grasping as those of some of the Old World monkeys. But many New World monkeys have long, grasping tails, which they use like an extra hand for picking up objects and for swinging from branch to branch.

ORNATE TITI have soft fur. Their long tails are not used for grasping and holding.

HUMBOLDT'S SAKI, though large and heavy, is too delicate for a pet.

RED HOWLER howls so loudly at night it can be heard for several miles.

MANTLED HOWLER is shy and does not live long after being captured.

MONKEYS

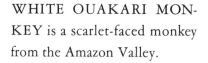

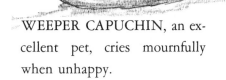

WHITE OUAKARI MONKEY is a scarlet-faced monkey from the Amazon Valley.

WEEPER CAPUCHIN, an excellent pet, cries mournfully when unhappy.

RED-BACKED SAKIS, of northern Brazil, live in pairs instead of larger groups.

GEOFFROY'S SPIDER MONKEY is kin to the more common Red-faced Spider Monkey.

The New World monkeys include the night monkeys, howlers, spider monkeys, woolly monkeys, capuchins (cap'-u-chin) and others. The capuchins are the best known. For years they were the favorite monkeys of organ-grinders and are still one of the best pet monkeys.

Marmosets are a separate group of monkeys, quite different from their other New World relatives. Some experts consider marmosets so different that they do not put them in the monkey groups at all. Most marmosets are small, about the size of squirrels, but with very different tails. They are attractive and are often kept as pets, though they are quite delicate. Marmosets are tree dwellers. Their long tails are not used for grasping like those of many New World monkeys, and only the big toes have the flattened nails that mark the monkey groups. The other toes have small claws.

- NAIL

CLAWS -

FOOT OF
SILKY MARMOSET
TWICE ACTUAL SIZE

Marmosets are a group of about 25 different kinds. Some are rare and seldom seen in zoos. Some have long silky hair, handsome ringed tails, or long tufts of hair near the ears. They are fond of insects, but also eat fruit, berries, seeds, nuts, and young shoots, just as other monkeys do.

COMMON MARMOSET has a long, ringed tail, and lives in the forests of Brazil.

GOLDEN, or LION-HEADED, MARMOSET, of the Amazon, has a golden-brown mane.

PIGMY MARMOSET, rare and delicate, can fit into the palm of your hand.

SILKY MARMOSET has long brown and golden fur with white ear tufts.

NEGRO TAMARIN has tusk-like canine teeth and long claw-like nails.

Monkeys are great fun to watch, but actually they do not act nearly as human as some people like to think. When a group of monkeys is caged together, the largest and strongest one takes over and becomes the "boss monkey." He gets first pick of food and seldom misses a chance to show he is boss. Monkeys live in constant fear of those that are stronger than they are.

BLACK APES

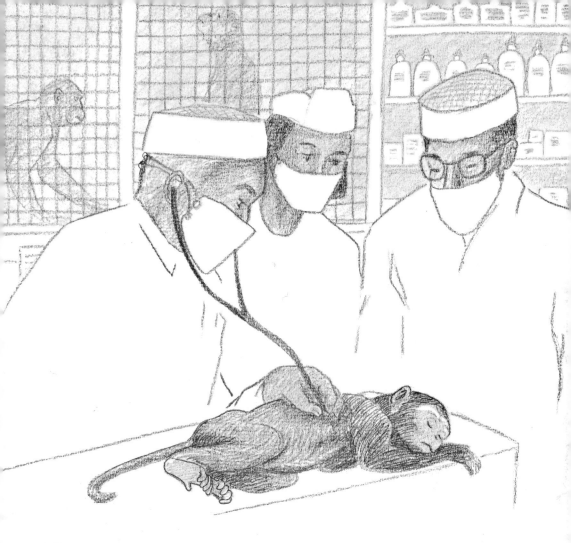

Though it is a mistake to think that monkeys are really like human beings, they are enough like us to make them very valuable for scientific experiments. By experimenting with

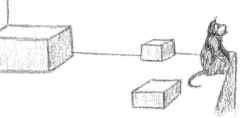

monkeys and apes, doctors learned how the virus that causes polio is spread. Monkeys have been used in studies of many diseases and to learn how different foods affect the body. Experiments on how monkeys learn to solve problems have helped us understand how our own minds work.

Records kept at zoos show that monkeys have a fairly long life span compared to other mammals. A mandrill has been known to live 27 years, a macaque up to 29, and a baboon to 45. But these may be special cases, and wild monkeys, on an average, may not live much over 10 or 12 years. And, as in human beings, the female monkeys seem to live longer than the males. Monkeys grow up more slowly than other animals their size. The average age at which most are old enough to mate and begin to raise young is from four to five years.

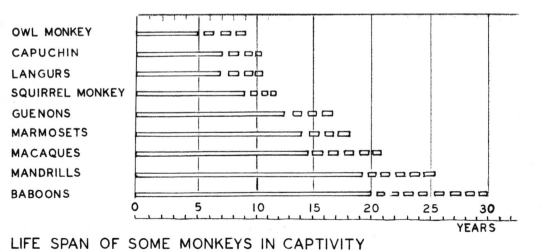

LIFE SPAN OF SOME MONKEYS IN CAPTIVITY

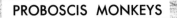

Scientists who have had a chance to study wild monkeys report that often one male, several females, and their young make up a family. The family may live and travel alone or may join with several other families. Thus a troop of monkeys may vary from four or five to a hundred or so.

The older, stronger males are in charge, though the females are able to care for themselves and their young. As young males grow up, the old male may drive them from the group or be driven away himself. The young males live alone for a time, but as they get stronger and bolder, they capture females and start families of their own. The families tend to keep enough to themselves so the young learn the family pattern from birth.

PATAS

JAPANESE MACAQUES

Monkeys have mated and raised young in many zoos. The young of small and medium-sized species are usually born about five or six months after mating. The exact time differs with different monkeys. The young of baboons and great apes grow inside the mother for seven to nine months before they are born. Most monkeys have but a single baby at a time. Marmosets often have twins and sometimes triplets. The mother nurses her young for at least six months, often for a year or longer. The father may or may not help care for the baby. He usually gives it some attention and may even carry it around.

COTTON-TOP MARMOSETS

OUAKARIS

Very soon after the baby monkey is born it is able to cling to its mother, and much of the time it does so. Even when it is old enough to run and play by itself, it leaps back to its mother at the first sign of danger. Monkey babies cling to their parents even during wild dashes through the trees or over the ground.

YELLOW BABOONS

Since people are so interested in monkeys, it is odd that more is not known about them. Scientific studies show that the blood of great apes fits into the same blood groups as ours does. There are distinct differences between the blood of New and Old World monkeys. One factor in monkey blood, called Rh factor—for rhesus monkey—also occurs in human blood.

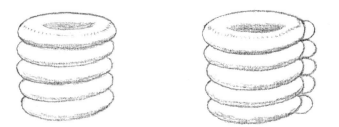

RH— AND RH+ RED BLOOD CORPUSCLES ARE EXACTLY ALIKE IN APPEARANCE. DOCTORS USE THE ABOVE TO INDICATE THE REAL DIFFERENCE BETWEEN THEM.

All monkeys' eyes look forward like ours, not to the side like those of a mouse or rat; and, like ourselves, most monkeys can see better by day than at night. There is proof that some monkeys, if not all, can tell shades of color. Because of the way their eyes are built, it seems likely that monkeys have the same stereoscopic, or three-dimensional, vision that we have.

OWL MONKEYS

Monkeys are more active by day. A few kinds, such as the night or owl monkey, prefer night life, and young monkeys often go out to play by moonlight. Monkeys sleep in a crouched position with their heads drooping, leaning against each other or against a branch. In cap-

43

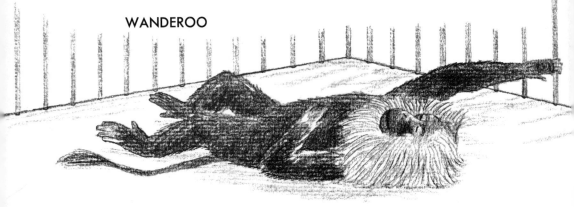

WOOLLY SPIDER MONKEYS

tivity, some will spread out on the floor of their cages, but most curl up on a branch to sleep.

Monkeys do not have as good a sense of smell as some other mammals. But odor is important to them, and they sniff at strange food and strange monkeys. A number of lemurs and New World monkeys have scent glands in their skins. That suggests that smell is one means by which some monkeys recognize each other.

WANDEROO

There are many things about monkeys you can discover for yourself by watching them at the zoo. Notice that most monkeys and apes drink by using their lips and cheeks as we do, but a few lap up water like cats.

Monkeys make a variety of sounds. Most common is a kind of chattering—very rapid and pleasant. While monkeys cannot speak, some of the sounds they make are always made under the same conditions, as when they are angry, happy, or afraid. Other monkeys seem to understand these sounds and recognize them. In a way, this is something like speech.

BROWN CAPUCHIN

CHINESE MACAQUES

Watch the changing look on monkeys' faces. You can easily tell whether they are content, curious, happy, or excited. If they are angry or afraid, they draw back their lips, show their teeth and grimace in a dozen ways. A man who has handled hundreds of monkeys tells me he never smiles when in the cage with them. Since monkeys draw back their lips and show their teeth when angry or afraid, a broad smile (which does the same thing to our faces) may seem to them to be a sign of fear. This man observed that when he smiled or laughed in the big cages, the monkeys, thinking he was afraid, quickly took advantage of this.

Watch monkeys grooming themselves and each other. They use their hands and sometimes their teeth, brushing and picking fur. Many people think the monkeys are looking for fleas, but monkeys groom their fur even when they are free of pests. They seem to enjoy grooming each other. Perhaps it is a sign of friendliness and affection. It is also said that while grooming they pick and eat bits of dead skin, because this adds salt to their diet.

WOOLLY MONKEYS

Watch monkeys eat. Feeding time may be fighting time also, as each tries to get his full share. See how well they handle their food. After they have satisfied their hunger they become more choosy and look for favorite bits.

MACAQUES

At some time or another everyone wants a monkey for a pet, but only a few people are lucky enough to get one. If you really want a pet monkey, ask yourself several questions first.

Does my family want a monkey as much as I do? It's true that no other pet (except a chimp) is more fun to train and play with. Monkeys are intelligent and full of mischief. But they also need special care, and protection against cold and disease. A monkey cannot be neglected. Everyone in the house should be willing to help before one is bought.

Do I have the time? A pet monkey needs much more attention than a goldfish or a hamster. You should feed it and train it yourself, and play with it every day. You may need to spend at least two or three hours daily with your pet, because most monkeys sold in pet stores are young and need a good deal of attention. Monkeys need personal attention just like babies. If you have the time, this is fun. Your pet learns to know you, respond to you, and, one might say, love you. But you must give it attention day after day without fail.

Can I afford it? Monkeys are not expensive. They cost no more than a pedigreed dog, but don't count on getting a young, healthy monkey for less than twenty-five dollars. Rare kinds sell for a hundred dollars or more. You must have a large, stout cage and you must buy the right food. Medical care may be needed if your pet becomes ill. All these are part of the total cost of having a pet monkey.

What kind of monkey should I get? Most people who have kept monkeys agree that a capuchin is a good pet for a beginner. It is of medium size, inexpensive, and fairly hardy. Young rhesus monkeys are more hardy and are nice, but as they grow they become big and powerful. Squirrel, spider, and woolly monkeys, and marmosets (though delicate) make good pets also, and more than a dozen other kinds have been raised in homes.

WHITE-THROATED CAPU-
CHIN is small, friendly, and
fairly hardy.

SQUIRREL MONKEYS, small
with long slim tails, may do well
in captivity.

RED-FACED SPIDER MON-
KEY needs climbing space and
protection from cold.

RHESUS MONKEY, widely
used in laboratories, is a good
pet when young.

NUTS

BREADS AND CEREALS

What do monkeys eat? They eat a great variety of foods—mostly vegetables, fruits, and nuts. Some like a bit of lean meat or chicken and are very fond of grasshoppers, crickets, or other insects. Some kinds live almost entirely on leaves. Like people, monkeys need a variety of foods. Give them all kinds of green leafy vegetables: lettuce, celery, kale, beet tops. Some nibble at fresh leaves or grass. All enjoy many kinds of fruits and nuts, including bananas and peanuts. In season, fresh fruits are best. Out of season try dried fruits (properly soaked) and frozen fruits. Monkeys will eat all kinds of bread. They like many of the breakfast cereals you eat and eggs and milk, too.

FRUITS

MEAT

VEGETABLES

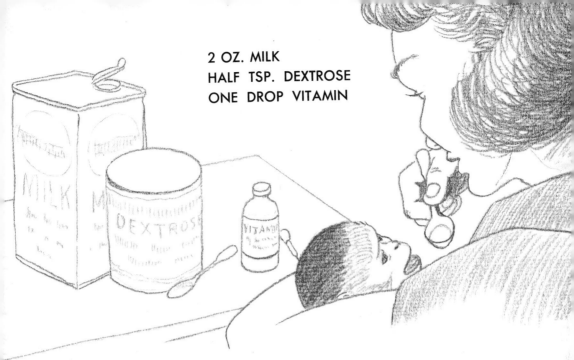

2 OZ. MILK
HALF TSP. DEXTROSE
ONE DROP VITAMIN

Young monkeys need milk for quite a long time, and grown monkeys are often benefited by it. Give them milk mixed according to a baby formula or add a half teaspoon of dextrose, or grape sugar, to two ounces of skimmed or homogenized milk. Mix in a small drop of tasteless vitamin concentrate, warm slightly, and serve. All zoos feed their monkeys extra vitamins to help protect their health. Keep the

amount small. Don't offer a pill made for a 160-pound man to a 2-pound monkey.

Some people prefer to feed monkeys twice a day. Others, who have the time, feed them more often. Babies and young monkeys should be fed frequently. Keep the total amount of food down to something that the monkey can soon finish. Leftover food in the monkey's cage may spoil and cause illness if eaten later.

What other care do monkeys need? Monkeys are mainly tropical, and unless the temperature is kept between 70 and 80 degrees, they may catch colds or even pneumonia. Some kinds like a nesting box into which they may crawl and sleep. They are smart enough to use a small blanket inside the box. Monkeys must not get too hot, either. A monkey should never be placed in strong summer sunlight, unless it is given some shade. Monkeys must be protected from drafts. Their cages must be kept dry and well ventilated. Avoid sudden changes in temperature, even with the few hardy monkeys. Monkeys are not easily housebroken. But if your monkey has the freedom of the house, you should certainly try to teach it good toilet habits.

HOT

COLD

DARK

LONESOME

How about a cage? Smaller monkeys need a cage 4 feet long, 4 feet wide, and 6 feet high. The extra height is for perches or branches on which the monkey can climb, sit, or swing. If a monkey is out of the cage much of the time for daily exercise, a smaller cage can be used at night. The cage should be made of material that is easily washed and kept clean. Experts recommend thin metal bars or heavy wire screening over a metal frame. The cage must be strong. A poorly made cage is a sure invitation for your curious pet to try to escape.

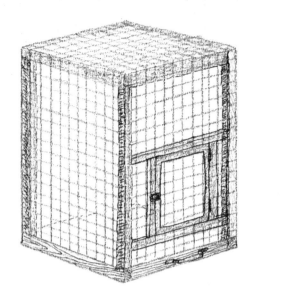

WIRE MESH OVER WOOD FRAME

PARROT CAGE

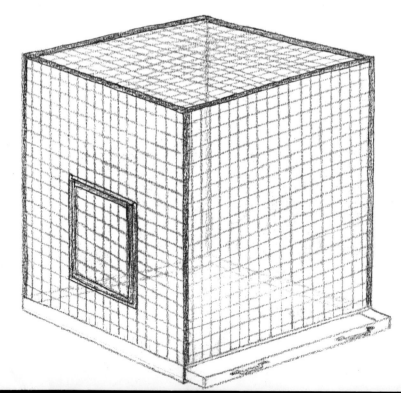

WIRE MESH OVER
IRON FRAME,
WITH SLIDING
TRAY FOR
CLEANING

If a pet monkey does escape, what you do depends on how long you have had it. A monkey that loves you is likely to follow you into the house or go into its cage if you call it and provide food. Keep strangers away. Chasing a monkey rarely does any good. If you have to trap one, try a simple box trap or use a fisherman's landing net.

Monkeys are such wonderful pets that it is too bad there are not enough of them to go around. Think of all the fun we would have if monkeys were as common as dogs or cats. But in that case there might be too many monkeyshines for comfort. Perhaps it is best for most of us to watch monkeys in zoos.